Bailey Sutton Dean

A Syllabus of Apostolic History

Bailey Sutton Dean

A Syllabus of Apostolic History

ISBN/EAN: 9783337404451

Printed in Europe, USA, Canada, Australia, Japan

Cover: Foto ©Lupo / pixelio.de

More available books at **www.hansebooks.com**

A SYLLABUS

—of—

APOSTOLIC HISTORY.

—by—

B. S. DEAN, A. M.,

Professor of History in Hiram College.

Introduction.

I. SOURCES.

1. BOOK OF ACTS—a continuation and completion of the Gospel narrative from Christ's ascension.

2. TWENTY-ONE EPISTLES. The first fourteen, with the possible exception of Hebrews, by Paul, mostly written in the later period covered by Acts, and fitting into its history.

3. THE APOCALYPSE OR REVELATION OF JOHN.

4. EXTRA-BIBLICAL TRADITIONS.

II. RELATIONS TO GOSPEL HISTORY

The "Gospels" contain christianity *in the germ*—the fundamental facts concerning Christ: his incarnation, earthly life, words, works, death, resurrection and ascension. But it is only in the germ. Without Acts and the Epistles we should be in the dark as to the actual reign of Christ. Jesus left much to the

direction of the apostles under the progressive inspiration of the Holy Spirit; cf. Jno. 14:26; 16:12-14; Acts 2:4; 10:28; yet Christ, not the apostles, the real actor. He the principal, they, only agents. In the first four books of the New Testament, the "beginning of the gospel" (Mark 1:1); in Acts, the gospel continued and completed. In the "gospels" John, Jesus, the twelve, the seventy, preach a "kingdom at hand;" in Acts Christ reigns and men enter his kingdom. In the gospels the apostles do not preach the Christhood, death, resurrection of Jesus, nor forgiveness in his name; in Acts they preach Christ in all lands in the fullness of his redemptive power. The apostles themselves did not, at first, grasp the full import of their world-wide commission. Hence, Jesus' directions in Luke 24:49. As the New Testament is the key and the completion of the Old, so the book of Acts is the key and the completion of the "gospels."

The Book of Acts.

INTRODUCTION.

I. THE TITLE.

Not part of original book. "The Acts of the Apostles" misleading. How many Apostles named in 1:13? How many appear later in Acts? Where does each drop out? cf. 8:14, 25; 15:7, 14. Truer title "ACTS OF APOSTLES." So manuscript B. Sinaitic manuscript has "ACTS."

II. AUTHOR.

1. WROTE A FORMER TREATISE; cf. 1:1; Luke 1:1-4.

2. COMMON AUTHORSHIP. (1) Fifty words, many medical terms, common to both, not found elsewhere in N. T. (1) Similar details and order in 1:1-9 and Luke 24:28-51.

3. AUTHOR A COMPANION OF PAUL; see "we" passages, 61:10-18; 20:5, 6, 13-15; 21:1-18; 27:1; 28:16, etc.

4. DISTINGUISHED FROM TIMOTHY AND OTHER COMPANIONS, 20; 4, 5.

5. EARLY UNIFORM TRADITION ASCRIBES BOTH BOOKS TO LUKE. On his race and occupation see Col. 4:10-14. His long association with Paul, especially the four years at Cæsarea and Rome would fit him for the task. "Father of church history."

III. DESIGN.

1. TRACE FULFILMENT OF LAST COMMISSION. cf. Matt. 28:19; Mark 16:15; Luke 24:47; Acts 1:8. (1) Beginning at Jerusalem, center of Jewish world. (2) Extending to Samaritans, half-way-house. (3) Transition to Gentiles through Peter. (4) Extension to Gentile centers through Paul to Rome, center of the world. The last occupies more than half the book. See Pulpit Com. and McGarvey, Acts, Int.

2. BOOK OF CONVERSIONS: See chaps. 2, 3, 4, 8, 9, 10, 13, 16, etc., etc.

3. "GOSPEL OF HOLY SPIRIT." Gospels relate personal ministry of Christ to ascension; Acts relate continuance of work under administration of Holy Spirit.

IV. CHRONOLOGY.

1. TWO UNDOUBTED DATES. (1) A. D. 44, Martyrdom of James and death of Herod, Acts 12; Josephus, Ant. XIX. 4:4. cf. V. 1; VIII. 2. (2) A. D. 60, Accession of Festus; Acts 25: 1; Jos. Ant. XX. 8:9-11.

2. DIVERSITY OF OPINIONS ON OTHER DATES. Following summary shows great diversity within narrow limits.

SYNOPSIS OF DATES ACCORDING TO DIFFERENT AUTHORS.

	Clark.	Usher.	Doddridge.	Hug.	Olshausen.	Eichhorn.	Hackett.	Meyer.	Wieseler.	Conybeare & Howson.	Lewin.	Schaff.	McGarvey.	Ewald.
Ascension of Christ	30	33	33	31	33	32	33	31	30			30	34	33
Stephen's Martyrdon	34	33	34			37	35	34	39	36	36	37	36	38
Paul's Conversion	35	35	35	35	35	37	36	35	40	37	37	37	36	38
Paul's First Journey to Jerusalem	38	38	38	38	38	40	39	38	43	39	39	40	39	41
Paul's Arrival at Antioch	42	43	42		41	42	42	43	44	44	43		43	44
Death of James and Herod	44	44	44	44	44	44	44	44	44	44	44	44	44	44
The Famine	44	44	44	44		44	45	44	45	45	44	44	44	45-6
Paul's Second Journey to Jerusalem	44	44	44		44	44	45	44	45	45	44	44	44	45-6
Paul's First Missionary Tour	45-8	45-6	45-6		45-9	45	46-7	45-7	45-7	48-9	45-6		45-9	48-7
Paul's Third Missionary Tour	50	52	49	52	52	52	50	52	50	50	48	50	50	52
Apostolic Council	50	52	49	52	52	52	50	52	50	50	49	50	50	52
Paul Begins Second Missionary Tour	51	53	50	53	52	53	51	52	50	51	53	51	50.	52
Paul's Fourth Visit to Jerusalem	54	56	54	55	55	56	54	55	54	54	54	54		55
Paul's Encounter with Peter at Antioch	54	52	50		55		54	52	54	50	54			
Paul Begins Third Tour	54	56	54	55	55	56	55	55	54	54	54	54	53	55
Paul's Fifth Visit to Jerusalem and Imprisonment	58	60	58	59	60	60	59	59	58	58	58	58	58	59
Paul's Imprisonment at Rome	61-3	63-5	61-3	62-4	63-5	63-5	61-2	62-4	61-4	61-3	61-3	61-3	61-3	62-4
Martyrdon of Paul	67		67	68	68	65	68	64	64	68	66	67	67	

V. GENERAL ANALYSIS.

PART FIRST.—Founding of the church in Jerusalem; I-II. A. D. 30.

PART SECOND.—Growth of the Church in Jerusalem; III-VII. A. D. 30-35.

PART THIRD.—Extension of the Gospel throughout Judea and Samaria and Transition to the Gentiles; VIII-XII. A. D. 35-45.

PART FOURTH.—Extension of the Gospel throughout the Gentile World through the labors of Paul; XIII-XXVIII. A. D. 45-63.

Part First.

FOUNDING OF THE CHURCH IN JERUSALEM; I-II.
A. D. 30.

I. PRELIMINARY MATTERS; I:1-26.

1. INTRODUCTION, 1-3. Theophilus, 1; cf. Luke 1:1. What "commandment?" 2; cf. Matt. 28:19, 20; Mark 16:15-18; Luke

2

24:44-49; John 20:19-23. "Through the Holy Ghost," 2; cf. Is. 61:1; Luke 4:18; ch. 10:38; Luke 3:22; 4:1.

2. THE FORTY DAYS, 4-3. Note the beginning place, 4; cf. Luke 24:49; Is. 2:3; Micah 4:2. What the "promise of the Father?" 4; cf. 5; Luke 3:16; 24:49; John 7:39; 14:16, 17. Why "restore the kingdom?" 6; cf. Matt. 3:12; 4:17; 13:24, etc.; 16:-19; 19:28; 20:21; Luke 24:21. Why geographical order of 8?

3. THE ASCENSION, 9-11. cf. Mark 16:19; Luke 24:41. Note points peculiar to each.

4. THE EIGHT DAYS OF WAITING, 12-26.

a. *Return to Jerusalem;* Why? cf. 12; Luke 24:49; v. 8. Distance of Olivet from Jerusalem? cf. 12; John 11:18.

b. *The company of Disciples.*

(1) The Apostles: compare the four lists.

Matt. 10:2-4.	Mark 3:16-19.	Luke 6:14-16.	Acts 1:13.
Simon Peter.	Simon Peter.	Simon Peter.	Simon Peter.
Andrew.	James.	Andrew.	James.
James.	John.	James.	John.
John.	Andrew.	John.	Andrew.
Philip.	Philip.	Philip.	Philip.
Bartholomew.	Bartholomew.	Bartholomew.	Thomas.
Thomas.	Matthew.	Matthew.	Bartholomew.
Matthew.	Thomas.	Thomas.	Matthew.
James, S. of Alpheus.	James.	James.	James.
Lebbeus, Thaddeus.	Thaddeus.	Simon the Zealot.	Simon the Zealot.
Simon the Canaanæan.	Simon the Canaanæan.	Judas, S. of James.	Judas, S. of James.
Judas Iscariot.	Judas Iscariot.	Judas Iscariot.	

(2) The women; name them, 14; cf. Luke 23:49, 55; 24:-10; Mark 16:1. Where Mary next named?

(3) His brethren; who? cf. Matt. 13:55; ch. 4:36, 37; Gal. 1:19. What change in them? cf. John 7:3-5.

(4) The 120, 15; cf. 1 Cor. 15:6.

c. *Expectant prayer,* 14; where? 13; cf. Luke 24:53; ch. 2:1, 2.

d. *Choice of Matthias,* 15-26; cf. 18,19; Matt. 27:38 as to (1) Manner of Judas' death, (2) Who bought the field, (3) origin of "Akeldama." Why only two put forward for apostleship? On qualifications of apostle cf. 1:8, 22; 26:16; 1 Cor. 9:1. Are those qualifications perpetual? On use of lot cf. Lev. 16:8; Josh. 7:14, 18; 18:10; Prov. 16:33.

II. DESCENT OF THE SPIRIT, II:1-13.

1. PENTECOST. What three O. T. names? cf. 1; Ex. 34:22; Lev. 23:15-17; Num. 28:26. What day of week? Lev. 23:15, 16.

2. EFFECT ON DISCIPLES, 2-4. What three manifestations? Why called a "baptism in spirit"? cf. 4; 1:5; Matt. 3:11, etc. See also 10:44-46; 11:16.

3. EFFECT ON MULTITUDE, 5-13. How many lands repre-

sented, and how account for so many? What the uppermost feeling? Why the charge of drunkenness?

III. THE SERMON OF PETER, 14-40.

I. Introduction. 14-21.

1. DEFENCE AGAINST MOCKERS: "third hour."
2. EXPLANATION: fulfilment of Joel, 2:28-32.

II. Theme---Jesus of Nazareth, 22.

III. Proposition: Jesus is Lord and Christ, 36.

IV. Proofs, 22-35.

1. JESUS' WORKS, 22.

(1) Seals of God's approval. (2) Well known to them.

2. JESUS' DEATH, 23.

(1) A plan of God. (2) Executed by wicked men.

3. JESUS' RESURRECTION, 24-32.

(1) The Christ to rise according to prophets. (2) Jesus *did* rise; twelve witnesses.

4. JESUS' EXALTATION, 33-35. Proved by

(1) Miracle of tongues. (2) Prophecy of David.

Carry out each argument as Peter would likely do. Why reserve main proposition to the end?

IV. THE RESULTS, 37-41.

1. A PUNGENT CONVICTION, 37a. What the agent and instrument? cf. John 16:7-11; Eph. 6:17.

2. A PRACTICAL QUESTION, 37b.

3. A PLAIN ANSWER, 38, 49. What meant by "gift of Holy Spirit"? John 7:39; ch. 5:32; Gal. 4:6. How does God call? 39, cf. John 6:44, 45; 1 Pet. 5:10. How many duties? Why faith omitted? How many promises?

4. AN EARNEST EXHORTATION, 40. How save themselves? How save from that generation?

5. INSTANT OBEDIENCE, 41. How many? Were all baptized? cf. 38. What facilities for baptizing? See McGarvey, Lands of the Bible 189-201.

6. STEADFAST CONTINUANCE, 42-47. What four items? Explain each. Was the community of goods permanent or compulsory? 45; cf. 5:4. Was the growth of the church spasmodic? 47.

NOTE.—(1) New guides—apostles of Christ. (2) New ordinances—baptism and Lord's supper. (3) New spirit of brotherhood.

The first Christian Pentecost an *isthmus*: on one hand the stormy Atlantic of Judaism and the Law; on the other, the peaceful Pacific of the Gospel of Jesus Christ.

Excursus on the Mission of the Holy Spirit.

INTRODUCTION.

1. WE MAKE TOO LITTLE OF THE MISSION AND POWER OF THE HOLY SPIRIT. Much of the Father and his love; of the Son and his words and work; far too little of Spirit. True, (1) does not speak of himself (John 16:13, 14), yet (2) a large fact and factor in gospel success.

2. THIS IS PRE-EMINENTLY THE 'DISPENSATION OF THE SPIRIT.

  a. *Appears rarely and at long intervals in O. T.*

  b. *Yet not wholly wanting*, cf. Gen. 1:2; 6:3; Ex. 31:3; I Sam. 10:10; 16:13; Ps. 51;11; I Pet. 1:11.

  c. *Prophetic glimpses of a coming spiritual illumination*, Is. 61:1; Joel 2:28.

d. *Jesus the embodiment of the divine spirit,* Luke 1:35; Matt. 3:16, 17; Acts 10:38; John 3:34.

e. *As marking the climax of spiritual development, Jesus was to baptize in the Holy Spirit.* (1) John's prediction, Matt. 3:11; Mark 1:8; Luke 3:16; John 1:33. (2) Jesus' own testimony, John 7:37-39; 14:15-17; 15:26; 16:7-15; Acts 1:4-5. (3) His last commission, Luke 24:49; Acts 1:8; Matt. 28:19.

I. MISSION TO THE CHURCH.

1. MODE OF COMMUNICATION.

a. *Immediate:* (1) At Pentecost, Acts 2:1-4. (2) At house of Cornelius, Acts 10:44-46. (3) The two cases classed together, Acts 11:15. (4) Identified as the baptism of the Holy Spirit, Acts 11:16. (5) Marked by supernatural endowments.

b. *Through laying on of Apostle's hands;* (1) Case of Samaritans, Acts 8:14-18; (2) Case of twelve disciples at Ephesus, Acts 19:6; (3) Both marked by supernatural powers.

Both the above modes may be classed as extraordinary.

c. *Ordinary, at baptism,* Acts 2:38. (1) Spirit itself given,

John 7:39; Acts 5:32. (2) Universal to Christians, Rom. 8:9; Gal. 4:6. (3) No evidence that it was accompanied with miracle working power.

2. OFFICE. (1) To supernaturally illuminate, John 14:26; 16:13-15; Acts 2:38. (2) Confer supernatural power, Luke 24:49; Acts 1:8; 1 Cor. 12:7-10. (3) Comfort, John 14:15-18. (4) Intensify our love, Rom. 5. (5) Help our prayers, Rom. 8:26, 27.

3. THE TRANSIENT AND THE PERMANENT.

a. *The Spirit's presence to be permanent.* Its *manifestations* variable; some passed away with the Apostolic age.

b. *Miraculous endowments to cease*, 1 Cor. 13:8; cf. Ch. 12.

c. *Moral and spiritual effects to abide*, Gal. 5:22, 23; cf. 1 Cor. 13:13. These effects outlived the miracle working power. They were *always* paramount. The accidental is transient; the essential never dies. Character and the forces that create it are the essentials. Hence,

d. *The prevalent term for the Spirit.* (1) Various terms as "Spirit of adoption," "of counsel," "of wisdom," "of truth," etc. (2) Holy Spirit or Ghost ninety times; as often as all others,

pointing to its effect on character. Its *greatest* triumph on Pentecost, the transforming influence on character of apostles. See Richardson, Office of Holy Spirit pp. 180, 181.

II. MISSION TO THE WORLD.

1. MODE OF WORKING.

a. *Indirect*, "World can not receive," John 14:17; 7:39.

b. *Mediate;* (1) Through the disciples, the church, John 16:7, 8; cf, Jesus' prayer, John 17:9, 20, 21. (2) By the word of truth or gospel, 2:37; Jas. 1:18; 1 Pet. 1:23.

2. OFFICE: Convict world of (1) Its own sin, John 16:7-11. (2) Jesus' righteousness, Ibid. (3) Coming judgment, Ibid.

III. CONTRASTS BETWEEN OLD AND NEW TESTAMENT GIFT OF SPIRIT.

1. IN OLD, OFFICIAL RATHER THAN PERSONAL; RELATED MORE TO OFFICE THAN CHARACTER. (1) Case of Judges, Judg. 3:10; 6:34; 11:29; 13:25. (2) Kings, 1 Sam. 10:10; 16:13. (3) Prophets, Num. 11:25-29; 2 Pet. 1:21.

2. IN N. T. BELONGS SOLELY AND UNIVERSALLY TO THE REGENERATE, Gal. 4:6; John 14:17. No room for Baalams,

Sauls or Caiaphases. It was before Pentecost that Judas betrayed and Peter denied.

3. UNITY OF NEW DISPENSATION A UNITY OF SPIRIT. Ancient Israel a unity; common ancestry, language, etc. Christ's Israel united to God and each other by one spirit, 1 Cor. 12:13.

Part Second.

GROWTH OF THE CHURCH IN JERUSALEM: III-VIII.

A. D. 30-35.

I. FIRST JEWISH PERSECUTION: III-IV.

1. THE LAME MAN HEALED, 3:1-11. What the hours of prayer? Why "look on us?" 4. Significance of "in the name?" 6; cf. 12, 16; 4:7, 10, 12.

2. PETER'S SECOND SERMON, 12-26. (1) Introduction: the miracle explained, 12-16. Purpose in 12? Why "God of Abraham?" Note series of stinging contrasts in 13-15. Whose faith in 16? cf. John 16:23, 24; Mark 16:17, 18. (2) Salvation offered, 17-26. Purpose in 17-18? How turn? 19; cf. 2:38. Parallel points in 2:38; 3:19. What the restoration of all things? 21. How does God bless men? 26.

3. ARREST AND DEFENCE OF PETER AND JOHN, 4:1-22.

a. *Arrest*, 1-4. What sect headed this persecution? 1; cf. 5, 6; 5:17. What the ground of hostility? 2; cf. 23:8; Luke 20:27. How many converts? 4.

b. *The examination*, 6-7. On Annas see Jos. Ant. xx. 9:1.

c. *Peter's defence*, 8-12. Note (1) skillful introduction; "good deed;" (2) bold avowal in 10; (3) *he* arraigns *them*, 11; (4) preaches to them 12.

d. *Private consultation*, 13-17. What ground for astonishment? 13. Why the consultation? 14, 16, 17.

e. *The prohibition and answer*, 18-22. What limitation to law of obedience to rulers? 19; cf. Rom. 13:1-7; ch. 5:29.

4. REPORT OF THE TWO AND PRAYER OF THE TWELVE, 23-31. Why the prayer? 23, 24. For what did they pray? 29, 30. How answered? 31.

5. UNITY AND LIBERALITY OF THE DISCIPLES, 32-37. What prayer fulfilled in 32? cf. John 17:21. What the source of the power in 33? Why Barnabas singled out? 36, 37.

III. DANGER FROM WITHIN, V:1-16.

1. SIN OF ANANIAS AND SAPPHIRA, 1-2. Why the adversative conjunction? 1. What their sin?

2. THE DETECTION, 3-4. How did Peter know? see 2 Kin. 5:25, 26. Why a lie to the Holy Spirit? On reference to Satan in 3 cf. John 8:44; 13:26, 27; 1 Chron. 21:1.

3. THE JUDGMENT, 5-10. Why the severity? cf. Matt. 23:13-39; ch 13:8-11. Whose act was it? Why no lamentations? See Lev. 10:6. Note, the first death of an apostle that of traitor and suicide; of disciples after Pentecost, covetous hypocrites. Monument against insincerity in the church.

4. THE EFFECT OF WHOLESOME DISCIPLINE, 11-16. What on the church? 11 On the work? 14.

III. SECOND JEWISH PERSECUTION, V:17-42.

1. SECOND IMPRISONMENT OF APOSTLES, 17-18. Who was high priest? 17; cf. 4:6. What sect active this time? What new cause of indignation? 4:18; cf. 5:28. How many apostles imprisoned?

2. RELEASE AND RENEWED ACTIVITY OF THE APOSTLES, 19, 21a. How and why released?

3. SECOND ARRAIGNMENT BEFORE THE SANHEDRIM, 21b-28. What danger to the rulers? 26; cf. 2:47.

4. PETER'S SECOND DEFENCE, 29:32. What points parallel to first defence? See 4:8-12. Why could not the apostles keep silence? 29; cf. 32:1-8; Matt. 28:19; ch. 26:16, 19; 1 Cor. 9:16. How was the Spirit a witness? 32; cf. 2:4; 4:29-31; Luke 12:12;

1 Pet. 1:12; Mark 16:20.

5. GAMALIEL COUNSELS MODERATION, 33-39. What the spirit of the council? 33. Who was Gamaliel? 34; cf. 22:3. Who Theudas and Judas? See Jos., Ant. xx. 5:1; xvii. 10:5. Pulpit Com. *in loco*; Smith's Bible Dict., etc. On Gamaliel's counsel, comp. Lowell—

"Truth forever on the scaffold, etc.

6. THE APOSTLES BEATEN AND RELEASED, 40-42. What the effect?

IV. THE FIRST DIVISION OF LABOR, VI:1-7.

1. COMPLAINT OF THE HELLENISTS, 1. Distinction between Hellenists and Hebrews? Were the widows a religious order? 6; cf. 9:41; 1 Tim. 5:3, 9, 10, 11, 16.

2. THE REMEDY; APPOINTMENT OF THE SEVEN, 2-6. What meant by serving tables? In what order did the church organization develop? What the function of congregation and of apostles in appointment of new officers? What the significance of laying on of hands? 6; cf. 13:3; 8:17-19; 19:6; 1 Tim. 5:22; Num. 27:22, 23. What significance in names of the seven? What their character?

3. THE RESULT; INCREASED LABORS AND FRUITS, 7. Why mention the priests?

V. THE FIRST CHRISTIAN MARTYR, VI:8-VII:60.

1. STEPHEN'S MINISTRY, 6:8-10. Was it confined to the work to which he was appointed? 8; cf. 10; 1:8; Luke 24:49; 1 Cor. 2:4, 5; Rom. 1:16. What class opposed him? How many synagogues mentioned? 9; cf. Myer and Pul. Com. *in loco* Cony. & How. i:66, 67. Did Paul dispute with Stephen? 9; cf. 21:39.

2. STEPHEN'S ARRAIGNMENT, 11-15. Was the prosecution honest? 11, 13. What measure of truth in the charges? 14; cf. case of Jesus, Matt. 26:61; John 2:19.

3. STEPHEN'S DEFENCE, 7:1-56.

a. *Introduction: their national origin*, 1-8. What Stephen's purpose in this section? At what place did the call come to Abraham? 2; cf. Gen. 12:1; 11:31. How old was Abraham when he entered Canaan? 4; cf. Gen. 11:26, 32; 12:4.

b. *A series of Saviors rejected, then accepted*, 9-41.

(1) Joseph, 9-16. How many went down to Egypt? 14; cf. Gen. 46:26-27. See Septuagint, of Gen. 46:20. Where was

Jacob buried? 15, 16; cf. Gen. 50:13. Did Abraham buy Shechem? 16; cf. Gen. 23:16-18; 33:18-20. Who was buried at Shechem? 16; cf. Josh. 24:32.

(2) Moses in Egypt, 17-36. Where did Stephen learn of Moses' education? Josephus Ant. ii. 9, 10.

(3) Moses in the wilderness, 37-41. Who was the prophet? 37; cf. Deut. 18:15, 18, 19; ch. 3:22-26.

c. *Israel's rejection by God*, 42, 43. Is the reference to earlier or later idolatries or both?

d. *The sanctuaries*, 44-50. Stephen's purpose in referring to them, 48, 49; cf. Is. 66:1; John 4:21-25.

e. ' *The application*, 51-53. Had they seen the *drift* of his speech? Had *loaded* his guns and fired them off at once. How had they resisted the Holy Spirit? 51; cf. 52.

4. STEPHEN'S DEATH, 54-60. Was his death legal? Purpose of the vision? What connection had witnesses with an execution? 58; cf. Deut. 17:7. What Saul's connection with the case? 58; cf. ch. 22:20. What Stephen's spirit? 60. His death must have deeply impressed Saul. St. Augustine wrote: "Si Stephanus non orasset Ecclesia Paulum non haberet."

4

Part Third.

EXTENSION OF THE GOSPEL THROUGHOUT JUDEA AND SAMARIA AND TRANSITION TO THE GENTILES: VIII-XII. A. D. 35-45.

I. THIRD JEWISH PERSECUTION, VIII:1-4.

What the origin? 1; cf. 11:19. Of what sect was the leader? 1, 3. What the effect? 1, 4. Why did the apostles remain at Jerusalem? How long since Pentecost? Had the gospel been preached outside Jerusalem? Who buried Stephen? 2; cf. 2:5.

II. EXTENSION TO SAMARIA, VIII:5-25.

1. PHILIP PREACHES IN THE CITY OF SAMARIA, 5-13. Did other scattered disciples preach? cf. 4. Are the labors of any others followed? cf. 11:19-21. What Philip was this? 5; cf. 1:13; 8:1; 6:5; 21:8. Who were the Samaritans? 2 Ki. 17:24-32. Was there Jewish blood in them? cf. 2 Chron. 30:1, 6, 7; 34:6; 35:17, 18; Jer. 41:5-8; John 4:12. What the order of the commis-

sion? 1:8. Why the Pentecostal features of Philip's work? 6-8, 12, 17. What previous ministry in Samaria? John, ch. 4.

2. MISSION OF PETER AND JOHN TO SAMARIA, 14-17. Object of the visit? cf. 11:22. What gift of Spirit? Why did not Philip bestow it?

3. SIN OF SIMON, 18-24. What connection with his previous practices? What "matter" in 21? What conditions of pardon to baptized believer? 22.

4. OTHER LABORS AND RETURN OF PETER AND JOHN, 25. Where did they preach? Were they called in question at Jerusalem for receiving Samaritans? cf. 11:1-3. Why not?

III. CONVERSION OF AN ETHIOPIAN OFFICER: [PRIVATE TRANSITION TO THE GENTILES?]
VIII:26-40.

1. PHILIP SENT TO SOUTH-WEST PALESTINE, 26. Meaning of desert? Why specified?

2. MEETS AN ETHIOPIAN OFFICER, 27-29. Where was Ethiopia? Of what race and religion was the officer? What encouragement to worship? Deut. 33:1; cf. Is. 66:1, 2. What supernatural agencies thus far?

3. PREACHES JESUS TO HIM, 30-35. Why Philip's question? What the key to O. T? What is it to preach Jesus?

4. BAPTISM OF THE EUNUCH, 36-38. What suggested baptism? Could it have been "sprinkle" (Is. 52:15)? Was he reading the Hebrew or Septuagint? 32, 33; cf. Is. 53:7, 8. Septuagint has "astonish" instead of "sprinkle" in Is. 52:15. Should we quote vs. 37?

5. PARTING OF PHILIP AND THE EUNUCH, 39-40. What the relation of joy to Christian assurance? 39. What other cities did Philip evangelize? Where does the history leave him? 40; cf. 21:8.

IV. CONVERSION AND EARLY LABORS OF SAUL,

IX:1-31. A. D. 35.

For other accounts cf. 22:1-6; 26:9-18; Gal. 1:11-24.

1. SAUL'S MISSION TO DAMASCUS, 1, 2. From whom? At whose desire? 1. To whom? 2. What authority had high priest in Damascus?

2. HIS VISION AND COMMISSION FROM CHRIST, 3-9. What would the light suggest? 3; cf. Ex. 3:2; 40:38; 1 Tim. 6:16; ch. 7:55. Why fall to ground? In what tongue was the voice? 2; cf.

26:14. Purpose of Jesus' appearance? 5; compare Saul's commission as given to Ananias (9:15), through Ananias (22:14, 15), before Agrippa (26:16, 18), and interpreted by Saul (Gal. 1:11, 12, 15-17; 1 Cor. 9:1). How reconcile 7 with 22:9? Why so long without food?

3. HIS BAPTISM, 10-18. Was Ananias the only disciple in Damascus? 10; cf. 2, 19, 25. How was Saul's question answered? 6; cf. 22:10, 16. What the nature of his blindness and its cure? How did he receive the Holy Spirit? 17, 18; cf. 2:38; 8:17.

4. SAUL'S EARLY LABORS, 19-31.

a. *First ministry in Damascus*, 19-22. How have access to synagogues? How his mission to Damascus known? 21; cf. 1, 2. What the burden of his preaching? 20, 22, cf. 2:36; 3:10, 12; 8:35; 17:2, 3.

[b. *Sojourn in Arabia*, Gal. 1:17.]

c. *Second ministry in Damascus*, 23-25. Were the "many days" (23), the same as 'certain days" of 19? cf. Gal. 1:17, 18; 1 Kings, 21:36-40. Who aided the hostile Jews? 23; cf. 2 Cor. 11:32, 33.

d. *First visit to Jerusalem*, 26-29. Saul's purpose in going

to Jerusalem? How long did he stay? cf. Gal. 1:18. Attitude of disciples toward him? 26; cf. 21. Who first trusted him? 27. How explain their distrust and Barnabas' confidence? cf. 4:36, 37; 11:22-26. "Original discoverer of Saul." What apostles did Saul meet at Jerusalem? Gal. 1:18, 19. Explain hostility of Hellenists, 29; cf. 6:9-11. Did Saul leave Jerusalem from fear? 29, 30; cf. 22:17-21. Why to Cæsarea and Tarsus? Why had the churches rest? 31. Difference between "edified" and "multiplied?"

V. LABORS OF PETER IN JUDEA, IX:32-43.

1. PETER AT LYDDA, 32-35. Were these events before or after Saul's visit to Jerusalem? Are all Peter's labors given? 32. Origin of disciples at Lydda? See 8:4, 40. What event here? 33, 34.

2. PETER AT JOPPA, 36-43. What led Peter to Joppa? What the intention and result of these miracles? 35-42; cf. Mark 16:20.

VI. [PUBLIC?] TRANSITION TO THE GENTILES.

A. *THROUGH PETER*, X:1-XI:18.

1. PREPARATION OF CORNELIUS, 10:1-8. Was Cornelius a

pagan gentile? Was his character such as you would expect in a frontier soldier? How account for it? What do you know of N. T. centurions? cf. Matt. 8:5-10; 27:54; ch. 27:1, 3, 43; 28:16. What did Cornelius ask? How supplied? How is the same lack supplied to-day?

2. PREPARATION OF PETER, 9-22. Was apostolic inspiration completed at Pentecost? cf. John 16:13; ch. 2:4, 39; 10:15, 38. State all the reasons Peter had for going to Cæsarea. Why the emphasis on Cornelius' devoutness? 22; cf. 2.

3. PETER'S MISSION TO THE GENTILE CORNELIUS, 23-48.

a. *Meeting of Peter and Cornelius*, 23-33 Who accompanied Peter, and why? 23; cf. 45:11, 12. How explain Cornelius' homage? 25. What law forbade a Jew to enter a Gentile's house? 28. How make four days? 30. Who were present, and what their mental attitude? 33; cf. 24, 27.

b. *Peter's Sermon*, 34-43. Sense of 34? cf. 35; Gal. 3:28. What did Cornelius know of Jesus? 37, 38. Of what was he ignorant? What contrasted offices in 42, 43?

c. *Double baptism of Gentiles*, 44-48. What the first baptism? 44; cf. 11:15, 16. What evidence of it? 46. Why the astonish-

ment? 45. What the second baptism? 47, 48. Why the unusual order of the two? Does baptism of Spirit make water baptism needless? 47, 48.

4. PETER'S DEFENCE OF THE CASE, 11:1-18. Who were the objectors? What ground of objection? Meaning of "the circumcision"? 2. State the points Peter makes to justify his course. What the result? How "granted repentance" to Gentiles? 18.

B. *THROUGH THE HELLENISTS*, XI:19-30:

1. WIDER EVANGELIZATION OF JEWS, 19. Connecting point with previous history? 19; cf. 8:4. Why the order of cities? 19.

2. HELLENISTS PREACH TO GREEKS, 20, 21. What probable difference between them and Cornelius?

3. MISSION OF BARNABAS TO ANTIOCH? 22-24. By whom sent and why? 22, 23; cf. 8:14.

4. SAUL BROUGHT TO ANTIOCH, 25, 26. By whom and why? Where was Saul? 25, 26; cf. 9:27. Greatest man in the church comes to greatest city in Asia. Starting point of wider work. What three new things in 26?

5. MISSION OF BARNABAS AND SAUL TO JERUSALEM, 27-30. Occasion of it? Spirit of it? Why such men chosen? When were elders chosen? 30.

VII. FOURTH JEWISH PERSECUTION: XII.

1. MARTYRDOM OF JAMES, THE BROTHER OF JOHN, 1, 2. Who this Herod? See Jos. Ant. xviii. 5, xix. 6:5-8; Hurlbut. Man. Bib. Geog. What prediction fulfilled? Matt. 20:20-28. Was the vacancy filled?

2. IMPRISONMENT AND RELEASE OF PETER, 3-19. Why arrest Peter? 3. What time of year? 3, 4. What precautions and why? 4; cf. 5:19-22, 23. Where did Peter go? 12. For what were they praying? 12; cf. 5. Why "his angel?" 15; cf. Matt. 18:10. Why "hold their place?" 17. What James and why named? 17; cf. 15:13. Why put keepers to death? 19.

3. PRIDE AND DEATH OF HEROD:—RETURN OF BARNABAS AND SAUL, 20-25. Relation of Palestine to Phœnicia, 20; bearing of 11:27, 28? What Josephus' account of Herod's death? Ant. xix. 8:2. Why did word of God grow? 24. Who was Mark? 25; cf. 12; 1 Pet. 5:11.

Part Fourth.

ENTENSION OF THE GOSPEL THROUGHOUT THE GENTILE WORLD UNDER THE LABORS OF PAUL. XII.-XXVIII. A. D. 45-63.

I. PAUL'S FIRST MISSIONARY TOUR, XIII.-XIV.

1. BARNABAS AND SAUL SET APART TO THE WORK, 13:1-3. What significance in order of names? 1. Difference in origin of this missionary movement and that from Jerusalem? 2; cf. 8:1, 4. When the original call? 2; cf. 9:15; 26:16-18; 6:6; 1 Tim. 4:14.

2. THEIR MISSION TO CYPRUS, 4-12, Who chose Cyprus? 4; cf. 4:36. Importance of Seleucia, Salamis, Paphos? To whom did they preach first? 5; cf. 14; 14:1, etc. John's office? 5. What John? 13; 15:37, 38; 12:12. Paul's purpose with Bar-jesus? 6-12. cf. 5:3. Why change in Paul's name and relative position? 9; cf. 2, 7, 13, 43, etc.

3. FROM PAPHOS TO ANTIOCH IN PISIDIA, 13-15. Trace the route. Why John's return? 13; cf. 15:38.

4. PAUL'S SERMON AT ANTIOCH, 16-41.

a. *Historical introduction*, 16-23. (1) God chose and exalted his people. (2) Delivered them from Egypt. (3) Gave them a land. (4) Gave them judges. (5) Gave them a king. (6) Removed him and raised up David. (7) From David came Jesus the Savior.

b. *Proofs that Jesus is the Savior*, 24-37. (1) John's testimony. (2) Jesus' rejection, which fulfilled prophecy. (3) His resurrection, attested by eye witnesses and by prophecy.

c. *Conclusion*, 38-41. (1) Remission and justification offered through Christ. (2) A word of warning. Resemblance to Stephen's and to Peter's sermon. What contrast? What chronological difficulty in 20? cf. Gal. 3:17; 1 Kings 6:1; Jos. Ant. viii. 3:1; see Myer and McGarvey *in loco*. Whence forty years? 21; cf. Jos. Ant, vi. 14:9. What contrast with the law? 39.

5. RESULTS OF THE FIRST SERMON, 42, 43. On Gentiles? 42. On Jews? 43. What third class?

6. PAUL'S SECOND SERMON AND RESULTS, 44-51. Character of audience? 44. Why envy of Jews? 45; cf. Luke 15:1, 2. What classes joined in the persecution? 50.

7. EVENTS AT ICONIUM, 14:1-6. Classes converted? 1. Source of faith? 1. Persecuting classes? 5. Who the instigators? 4.

8. EVENTS AT LYSTRA AND DERBE, 7-21. Source of cripple's faith? 9. What shows a provincial population? 11. Why call Barnabas Jupiter? Who stoned Paul? 19. What witness of his sufferings?

9. THE RETURN TO ANTIOCH, 21:28. What the order of return? What additional services to each church? 22, 23; cf. Titus 1:5. What new preaching point? 25.

II. INTERVAL BETWEEN THE FIRST AND SECOND TOURS: XV. 1-29.

1. CONTROVERSY ON CIRCUMCISION, 1-29.

a. *Origin of the question*, 1-5. How differ from issue raised about Cornelius? 5; cf. 11:3. Who carried it to Jerusalem? 2; cf. Gal. 2:1. Was it an appeal from decision of a church to decision of a council? To whom did they report? 4.

b. *Council of apostles and elders*, 6-29. How many meetings? cf. 4-6; Gal. 2:2. Paul's reasons for going? 2; Gal. 2:2. Note order of speeches:

(1) Much disputing by—nobodies. (2) Speech of Peter: state his points. (3) Speeches of Barnabas and Paul. Why the old order of names? 12, 25; cf. 13:46, 2. Why refer to miracles? (4) Speech of James. How does it differ in character from the others? Why the specifications in 20? Point of 21. Who made the final decision? 22; cf. 25, 28. Why Judas and Silas sent?

c. *Return of Paul and Barnabas to Antioch*, 30-35. The feeling at Antioch? Had the trouble originated with Antioch disciples? 1. Did Silas and Judas return to Jerusalem?

d. [*Visit and dissimulation of Peter*, Gal. 2:11-14.]

e. *Quarrel of Paul and Barnabas*, 36-39. Reasons for Paul's objections to Mark and Barnabas' preference? 38; cf. Col. 4:10. Why did Paul afterward change his opinion? cf. 2 Tim. 4:11.

III. PAUL'S SECOND MISSIONARY TOUR: XV:40-XVIII:22.

1. REVISITS OLD FIELDS, 15:40-16:5. What change of companions? 40. Primary purpose of tour? 15:36, 41; 16:4, 5. When and by whom were churches in Syria and Cilicia planted? 41; cf. 9:40; 11:19; Gal. 1:21. Fields of the first tour revisited?

16:1. What known of Timothy's parentage and education? 1; cf. 1 Tim. 1:2; 2 Tim. 1:5; 3:15. Why circumcise Timothy when he had refused to circumcise Titus? 3; cf. Gal. 5:2-4.

2. NEW FIELDS IN ASIA MINOR, 6-8. What new fruits? 6; cf. 18:23; see also Epistle to Galatians. What limitations, how and why? 6, 7.

3, PAUL AT PHILIPPI, 9-40. What larger plans for Paul? 9. What connection with 6, 7? Who joined the company at Troas? How long the voyage? 11. Meaning of "colony"? 12.

a. *Conversion of Lydia*, 13-15. What implied in last clause of 12? What inference from place and character of meeting? 13. How and in what sense did God open Lydia's heart? 14. Any infants baptized? 15; cf. 13, 40.

b. CONVERSION OF A JAILOR. What a spirit of divination? 16, 18. Why grieved with the maid's testimony? 18; cf. Mark 1:34. What the real complaint of her masters? 19-21. Why the terms Jews and Romans? 20, 21. Motive of magistrates? 22. Why the purposed suicide? 27. Why the question in 30? Were any infants baptized? 33; cf. 32, 34. Was the baptism in the prison? 30; or the house? 34. Why the message of the

magistrates? 35. Why Paul's refusal? 37. In what sense was he a Roman? 37; cf. 21:26-28. Who of Paul's company remained at Philippi? 40; cf, 16:10; 17:1, 10.

4. PAUL AT THESSALONICA, 17:1-9. Why pass two cities to stop at Thessalonica? 1. What Paul's method with Jews? 2, 3. Which class of converts more numerous? 4. Why assault house of Jason? 6, 7. Why the zeal for Cæsar? 7; cf. Luke 23:2; John 18:12. Ground of accusation in 6? Any miracles? 1 Thess. 1:5. How supported? 1 Thess. 2:9; Phil. 4:15, 16.

5. PAUL AT BEREA, 10-14. Why the night journey? 10; cf. 26:31. Force of "therefore" in 12? Was it the original plan to go to Athens? 15. Why leave Silas and Timothy behind? 14. Why to follow so soon? 15, 16.

6. PAUL AT ATHENS, 16-34.

a. *First Work at Athens*, 16-21. Force of "full of idols"? 16. See C. & H. i. 357, 363. Describe classes and places in 17, 18. Point of charge in 18? On the Areopagus see C. & H. i. 346, 354, 376. Did Timothy join him? 16; cf. 1 Thess. 3:1, 2.

b. *Paul's Sermon on Mars' Hill*, 22-31.

1. INTRODUCTION: THEIR REVERENCE, 22, 23. Meaning of

superstitious"? 22. How shown? 23. What his theme? Why thus introduced?

    II. GOD'S RELATION TO THE UNIVERSE, 24-28.

    1. *To material world*, 24. What assumption, deduction and local allusion?

    2. *To men*, 25-28. What three main propositions? What inferences? What local allusion? 25.

    III. THE NATURE OF GOD, 29. Inferred from what? What local allusion?

    IV. CONCLUSION, 30, 31. Sense of overlooked? 30; cf. 14:16. What motive to repentance? 30. Bearing of the resurrection of Jesus? 31; cf. 10:41, 42. Where find germs of this sermon? see 14:15-17.

    c. *Results at Athens*, 32:34. Why so meagre? cf. 1 Cor. 1:21-23; 2:1-5. Why name Dionysius and Damaris?

    7. PAUL'S LONG STAY AT CORINTH, 18:1-17.

    a. *First Labors*, 1-4. Differences between Athens and Corinth? See C. & H. i. 383. State of Paul's mind? 1 Cor. 2:1. Means of support? 3; cf, 1 Cor. 4:12. Trace Aquila's movements, 1. Was he a disciple? cf. 26.

b. *Arrival of Silas and Timothy: Increased Labors*, 5-17. Movements of Silas and Timothy? 5; cf. 17:15; 1 Thess. 3:1, 2. What change on Timothy's arrival and why? 5, 6; 1 Thess. 3:6, 7. Name some converts at Corinth, 8; cf. 1 Cor. 1:14-16. Why the vision? 9, 10. Who was Gallio? 13. What charge of the Jews? 13. What law and worship? Why the case dismissed? 17.

First Epistle to Thessalonians.

1. TIME AND PLACE OF COMPOSITION, cf. 1:1; 3:6-8; Acts 18:5. At Corinth on second tour, soon after Timothy's arrival, Cir. A. D. 53.

2. GENERAL ANALYSIS.

a. *Personal: Recalls past*, 1. (1) While with them, 1-2; 16. (2) Since his departure, 2:17-3:13.

b. *Didactic and Hortatory*, ch. 4-5.

3. HISTORICAL ITEMS. (1) Silas and Timothy with him, 1:1. (2) Had he worked miracles? 1:5. (3) Thessalonica a gospel center, 1:7, 8. (4) Majority had been idolaters, 1:9; cf. Acts 18:1-4. (5) How was Paul supported? 2:9; cf. Phil. 4:16. (6) Had sought to visit them, 2:17, 18. (7) Why had he sent

Timothy? 3:1, 2, 5. (8) Effect of Timothy's return? 3:6-8. (9) What warnings? 4:3, 6, 11, 12. (10) Troubled over Christ's second coming, 4:13-5:2. What is difficulty? 4:13. (11) Was the church organized? 5:12. (12) Were there spiritual gifts? 4:19, 20.

Second Epistle to Thessalonians.

1. TIME AND PLACE. (1) Silas and Timothy still with him, 1:1. (2) Did not leave Corinth with him, Acts 18:18. (3) Tenor of letter similar to 1 Thess. Probably written late in stay at Corinth.

2. GENERAL ANALYSIS.

a. *Consolations under Renewed Persecutions*, ch. 1.

b. *Instructions and Exhortations concerning the Second Coming of Christ*, ch. 2.

c. *Closing Exhortations and Instructions*, ch. 3.

3. HISTORICAL ITEMS. (1) Still persecuted but growing, 1:3, 4. (2) Still troubled over Christ's coming, 2:1-4. (3) Disorderly persons still among them, 3:6-15. (4) Meaning of tradition? 2:15; 3:6. (5) Token of Paul's epistles? 3:17. Why mention it? cf. 2:2.

8. PAUL'S RETURN TO ANTIOCH, 18:18-22. Who accompanied, and who remained? Whose vow? 18; cf. C. & H., i, 422. On vow see Num. 6:5, 18; ch. 21:24; 1 Cor 9:20. What hopeful feature at Ephesus? 20. Why not remain? Why leave Priscilla and Aquila? Did he visit Jerusalem? 21, 22.

IV. PAUL'S THIRD MISSIONARY TOUR,

XVIII:23-XX:26.

1. SECOND TOUR IN GALATIA AND PHRYGIA, 18:23; cf. 1 Cor. 16:1

2. APOLLOS AT EPHESUS, 24-28. Significance of his birthplace? See C. & H. i. 10-18, 37. What defects in his preaching and how corrected? 25, 26. What later notice of him? 27, 28; cf; 1 Cor. 1:12.

3. PAUL'S LONG STAY AT EPHESUS, 19:1-20:1. On Ephesus see C. & H. ii. 69-75.

a. *Rebaptizes Twelve Disciples*, 1-7. Why his question? 2; cf. 6. Were such endowments universal in the church? cf. 1 Cor. 12:4-13. Christian baptism differed from John's: It was (1) in name of Christ, 5; (2) connected with gift of Holy Spirit.

b. *Preaches Three Months in the Synagogue*, 8.

c. *Preaches Two Years in School of Tyrannus.* Why the change? 9. What advantage? 10.

d. *Conflict with Jewish Exorcists*, 13-20. On exorcists see C. & H. ii. 21-25; Jos. Ant. viii. 2, 5. Implication of "showed their deeds"? 18. Why burn their books?

e. *Plans Further Journeys*, 21-22. Last glimpse of Timothy? 22; cf. 18:5. Who was Erastus? 22; cf Rom. 16:23.

First Epistle to the Corinthians.

1. TIME AND PLACE OF COMPOSITION. Cf. 16:1-12; Acts 19:20; 20:1. (1) Had been in Galatia. (2) Was going through Macedonia to Greece. (3) Would tarry at Ephesus. (4) Because of "open doors" and "many adversaries." Written at Ephesus after the conflict with exorcists and before the mob.

2. HISTORICAL ITEMS. (1) Church rich in spiritual gifts, 1:4-7; 12:1-11, 28-31; 14:1-33. (2) Divided over leaders, 10-15; 3:1-6. Were the persons named real leaders? 1:12; cf. 4:6. (3) Tolerating fornication, 5:1-3; 6:15-20. (4) A previous letter on same subject, 5:9. (5) Lawsuits between brethren, 6:1-7. (6) They had written Paul on a question of marriage and di-

vorce, 7:1-17. Who brought their letter? 1:11; 16:17. (7) Question about heathen feasts, 8:1-13. What conclusion? 13. (8) Some denying Paul's apostleship, 9:1-6. (9) Perverting the Lord's supper, 11:17-34. (10) Jealousy over spiritual gifts, 12:21-31; 14:1-3; 18, 19, 23-25. (11) Some denying resurrection, 15:12. Who? cf. 23:6-8. Why devote so much time to it? 13-19. (12) Paul was making collection for the poor, 16:1-4. (13) Timothy's movements, 16:10, 11; cf. Acts 18:5; 19:22. (14) Apollos at Corinth (16:12), Aquila and Priscilla at Ephesus, 16:19.

THE COLLECTION.

1. *Objects*, Gal. 2:10; 24:17. (For earlier collection see Acts 11:27-30. (1) Relieve poor at Jerusalem. (2) Conciliate Jews and cement Jewish and Gentile Christians.

2. *Where collected*, 1 Cor. 16:1; 2 Cor. chaps. 8, 9.

3. *Means*, (1) Paul's personal appeals. (2) His letters. (3) Other agents, as Titus, 2 Cor. 8:6, 16, 17; 12:18; and the "brother," 8:18, 19, 22, 23; 12:18.

4. *Motives*, (1) Love to Christ, 2 Cor. 8:8. (2) Example of Christ, 2 Cor. 8:9. (3) Emulation, 9:1, 2. (4) Regard to his

feelings, 2 Cor. 9:2-4. (5) Hope of reward, 9:6-10. (6) Glorify God, 9:11-15.

5. *Practical Directions*, (1) Lord's Day contribution, 1 Cor. 16:1. (2) Messengers to carry the gift, 1 Cor. 16:3, 4.

f. *Mob of silversmiths?* 23-41. On temple of Diana see C. & H. vi. 73-77. Main motive of the silversmiths? 24-25, 27. What appeal to the populace? 27, 38. Object of the Jews? 33. Why Alexander not heard? 33, 34. State the arguments of the town clerk, 35-40.

4. PAUL'S SECOND TOUR IN MACEDONIA AND GREECE, 20:1-3. What stop on the way? cf. 1 Cor. 2:12, 13. What work in Macedonia? How far to the northwest did Paul probably go? Rom. 15:19. How long in Greece? 3. What change of plans? 3; cf. 19:21.

Second Epistle to the Corinthians.

1. TIME AND PLACE OF COMPOSITION. (1) After the mob at Ephesus, 1:8-10. (2) After reaching Macedonia, 2:12, 13; 7:5. (3) Before reaching Greece, Acts 20:1, 2. Probably written at Philippi.

2. HISTORICAL ITEMS. (1) Alludes to mob at Ephesus,

1:8, 9; cf. Acts 19:30. (2) An intended visit to Corinth, 1:15-17. Why not made? 1:23; 2:1, 2. (3) The case of incest, 2:4-11; 7:4-16. What change in Paul's feelings, and why? (4) Why Paul's disappointment at Troas? 2:12, 13; cf. 7:5-7. (5) Progress of the collection, chs. 8, 9. (6) Defends his apostleship, chs. 10-12. Grounds of attack? 10:10; 11:7, 8. What the signs of his apostleship? (7) Means ot support at Corinth, 11:7-12. How agree with Acts? 18:3; cf. 11:9; Acts 18:5. (8) Paul's previous sufferings, 11:24-33. How many of them recorded in Acts?

Epistle to the Galatians.

1. TIME AND PLACE OF COMPOSITION. (1) Soon after leaving them. (2) Was over two years at Ephesus. (3) Spent three months at Corinth. (4) Written at Ephesus or Corinth. The "so soon" (1:6) favors Ephesus; striking similarities to Romans favors Corinth.

2. HISTORICAL ITEMS. (1) Galatians being perverted, 1:6-9. Nature of the perversion? 3:1-3; 4:21; 5:1-4. Who the perverters? 6:12-13; cf. Acts 15:1. (2) How Paul learned the gospel, 1:1, 11, 12, 15-20. Why insist on it? (3) Paul's sojourn

in Arabia, and return to Damascus, 1:17. Why state the fact? (4) His visits to Jerusalem, 1:18, 19; 2:1-9. Why refer to these visits here? Which visit referred to in Acts 15:1? From what event does he reckon in 1:18 and 2:1? Why mention Titus? 2:3-5 (5) Paul rebukes Peter, 2:11. Ground of it? 12. Who else involved? 13. (6) Paul's physical infirmity, 4:13, 14; cf. 2 Cor. 12:7-9; ch. 4:15. (7) Paul his own secretary, 6:11.

Epistle to the Romans.

1. TIME AND PLACE OF COMPOSITION. Going to Jerusalem with contributions, 15:25, 26; cf. 20:3; 24:17. Gaius his host, 16:23; cf. 1 Cor. 1:14. Written at Corinth on third tour.

2. HISTORICAL ITEMS. (1) Their faith famous, 1:8; 16:19. (2) Paul's purpose to visit them, 1:9-15; 15:23, 24, 32; cf. Acts 19:21; 23:11. What further plans? (3) Further account of Priscilla and Aquila, 16:3, 4. Trace their movements, Acts 18:1, 18, 24-26; 1 Cor. 16:19; Rom. 16:3. What service to Paul? 16:4. Why dare return to Rome? (4) Large number of eminent members, 16:5-15. (5) Paul fears for his visit to Jerusalem, 15:30-32. Why? (6) Paul's companions at Corinth, 16:21-23. Which his secretary? 16:22. Who were his kinsmen

at Rome? 16:7, 11, 13. At Corinth? 16:21. Who bore the epistles? 16:1, 2.

NOTE.—The earlier epistles of Paul fall into pairs: 1. I. and II. Thessalonians, written at Corinth; leading theme, *Second coming of Christ*.
2. I. and II. Corinthians, just before and soon after leaving Ephesus, *Abuses in the Church at Corinth*.
3. Galatians and Romans, at Corinth, *Principle of Justification*.

5. THE RETURN TRIP TO JERUSALEM, 20:4-21:16.

a. *Last Days in Macedonia*, 20:4-6a. Who his companions? 4. What city did Paul re-visit? 6. Who joined him there? 6. How long the voyage to Troas? 6; cf. Acts 16:11.

b. *A Week at Troas*, 6b-12. Why so many days? 7. What inference as to Lord's Supper?

c. *The Journey to Miletus*, 13-16. Trace movements of Paul and of his company? Why pass by Ephesus?

d. *Address to Ephesian Bishops*, 17:38.

I. Reviews his Three Years' Ministry, 18-21. 1. The spirit of it, (1) Humble, (2) Faithful, (3) Diligent. 2. The theme of it, (1) Repentance toward God, (2) Faith toward Christ.

II. Forecasts his Future, 22-27. 1. Going to Jerusalem,

2. Shadows of impending imprisonment. 3. An immovable purpose. 4. A sorrowful expectation. 5. An appeal to his record.

III. Future of Ephesian Church, 28-35. 1. Duties of the Bishops. 2. Perils ahead. 3. Exhortation based on example. 4. Apostolic benediction. 5. Unselfish service and divine example.

IV. A Sorrowful Farewell, 36-38.

e. *The Voyage from Miletus to Cæsarea*, 21:1-80. What change of ship? Which side of Cyprus? 3. Why so solemn parting at Tyre? 5; cf. 4. Origin of churches at Tyre and Ptolemais? 7; cf. 11:19.

f. *The Sojourn at Caesarea*, 8b-16. Which Philip? 8; cf. 6:5; 8:49. Meaning of "prophesy?" 9. On Agabus, 10, 11; cf. 11:27, 28. Why Paul so determined? Why "will of the Lord?"

g. *Paul's Reception at Jerusalem*, 15-26. What important "baggage?" 15. Who Paul's host? What James and what his office? 18; cf. Gal. 1:19; 2:9, 12; ch. 15:13, 19. Were Paul's alms accepted? What class to be conciliated? 20. What ground of hostility? 21. Was charge true? Gal. 5:4; cf. ch.

15:11. Did Paul's course exceed the limits of wise expediency? cf. 1 Cor. 9:19-22. Did it succeed?

V. PAUL'S IMPRISONMENT AT JERUSALEM, XXI:27-XXIII:30.

1. MOBBED BY JEWS, 21:27-30. What class of Jews? 27. Were charges true? 28, 29; cf. 24:12, 13.

2. ARRESTED BY ROMAN CAPTAIN, 31-46. Difference between "captains" of 31 and centurions of 32? Why bind Paul? 33; cf. 38. Why the surprise? 37. On the 'Egyptian" see Jos. Ant. xx. 8:6; Wars ii. 13, 5. Why different languages? cf. 37, 40; 22:2.

3. ADDRESSES THE MOB ON THE STAIRS, 22:1-21.

a. *Natural Affiliation with Them*, 1-5. (1) A Jew by blood. (2) Foreign born, yet, (3) Educated at Jerusalem. (4) A fierce persecutor of Christians.

b. *Reason for Change—His Conversion*, 6-16. Why the particulars in 12? Why omit mission to Gentiles in this section? cf. 14, 15; 26:16-18.

c. *His Mission to the Gentiles*, 17-21. Where else related? 18, 21; cf. 9:28-30.

4. RESULTS OF PAUL'S SPEECH, 22-29. What the offensive word? 23; cf. 21. Object of binding? 25; cf. 24. What different ways of obtaining Roman citizenship? See McGarvey, ii. 221, note.

5. PAUL BEFORE THE COUNCIL, 22:39-23:10. At whose desire? 22:30. Meaning of good conscience? 23:1; cf. 26:9. Was Paul's retort justifiable? 3; cf. Mark 3:5; Matt. 23:13-33; ch. 13:8-11; Eph. 4:26. Was Paul's purpose honorable in 6?

6. PAUL'S VISION IN THE CASTLE, 11. Purpose of vision? cf. 19:21. Rom. 15:22-24; 30-32. Did the foreknowledge make human precaution unnecessary? cf. 17.

7. A CONSPIRACY AGAINST PAUL, 12-22. How many parties to the plot? 12-15. Why did Paul not tell the captain? 17. What inferences from 19, 22?

8. PAUL SENT TO CÆSAREA, 23-35. Distance to Cæsarea? What courses open to Lysias? Does his letter color any part of the affair? Why send the soldiers back? 32. Why the question in 34? On Cæsarea cf. Jos. Ant. xv. 9, 6. C. & H. ii. 279-252.

VI. PAUL'S IMPRISONMENT AT CÆSAREA, XXIV-XXVI.

1. PAUL'S TRIAL BEFORE FELIX, 24:1-23. On Felix see Jos. Ant. xx:7, 1.

a. *The Prosecution*, 1-9. Who the accusers? 1, 9. What charges, general and specific? . 6. What proofs?

b. *Paul's Defence*, 10-23. Compare Paul's introduction with Tertullus' 2-4, 10. How make the twelve days? 11; cf. 21:15, 17, 18, 27; 23:31, 32; 24: . Which charge denied? 12, 18. Which confessed? 14. Why emphasize the resurrection? 15, 21; 23:6. What Felix's present decision and on what based? 22, 23.

2. PAUL'S SERMON BEFORE FELIX AND DRUSILLA, 24-27. On Drusilla see Jos. Ant. xviii. 5, 4; xx. 7, 1, 2. Object of Drusilla? What phase of the faith presented, and why? 25. How harmonize Felix's terror with 26? On succession of Festus see Jos. Ant. xx. 8, 9.

3. PAUL'S TRIAL BEFORE FESTUS, 25:1-12. Why go to Jerusalem? 1. Why keep Paul at Cæsarea? 3, 4. How reconcile 4 with 9? Why appeal to Cæsar? 10. Who had the right of appeal to Cæsar? 10, 12, 21, 25. Effect of appeal?

4. PAUL BEFORE AGRIPPA, 25:13-26:32.

a. *Arrival of Agrippa and Bernice*, 13. Who were they? See Jos. Ant. xix 9; xx.7; C. & H. ii. 272. Purpose of their visit?

b. *Paul's Case Stated to Agrippa*, 14-22. Why Agrippa's interest in the case? 18, 19, 22; cf. 26;1, 2. Meaning of religious? 19; cf. 17:22.

c. *The Audience*, 23-27. How compare with that on Mars' Hill? 23; cf. 17:18, 19. Why state the case again?

d. *Paul's Defence*, 26:1-29.

I. Introduction, 1-3. What gesture? 1; cf. 13:16; 21:40; 29. Where the emphasis in 2, and why? cf. 3.

II. The Charges Inconsistent, 4-7. (1) He was a Jew, 4; (2) and a Pharisee, 5; (3) believed the promises, 6; (4) which Jews believed.

III. His Course was Directed by God, 8-22a. (1) Had been prejudiced against Jesus, 9-11. (2) Had seen the glorified Jesus, 12-15. (3) Had been sent by Him to the Gentiles, 16-22a.

IV. Proofs from Prophecy, 22b, 23. (1) The Christ to suffer, (2) to rise from the dead, (3) to be the light of the people (Jews) and the Gentiles.

v. *Double Interruption and Conclusion*, 24:29. Why Festus' opinion? 24; cf. 17:22. At whom is Paul aiming? 26. What point the climax? 27; cf. 22, 23. Was Agrippa's remark ironical? 28. How did Paul treat it? 29. Difference between Agrippa's interruption and that of Festus?

d. *The Conference and Decision*, 30-32. Why did Paul not continue his speech? What impression had he made? To what was Paul's protection due? 32; cf. 25:9, 10; 24:27; 22:24-29.

VII. PAUL'S VOYAGE TO ROME, XVII:1-XVIII:16a.

1. THE RUN TO FAIR HAVENS, 27:1-8. Who the company? 1, 2; cf. 37. What ship? What points touched? 3, 5. What events at each? Which side of Cyprus, and why? 4; cf. 21:3. What change of direction at Cnidus?

2. THE RUN TO MELITA, 9-44.

a. *Discussion about Continuing the Voyage*, 9-12. Why reference to the fast? 9. Why Paul's judgment? 10. Why leave Fair Havens? 12.

b. *The Storm*, 13-20. Direction of the wind? What danger? 17. What expedients for safety?

c. *Helpful Services of Paul*, 21-38. The source of Paul's

help? 22, 23, 25. How reconcile 22 with 10? What indications of land? 27, 28. What unusual mode of anchoring? 29. What Paul's second service? 31. His third service? 34, 35. Why lighten the ship again?

d. *The Wreck and Escape,* 39-44. What change in sail, and why? 40; cf. 17. Why beach the ship? What new evidence of Paul's influence? 42, 43.

3. THE WINTER IN MELITA, 28:1-11a. On site of wreck see C. & H. ii. 341-343. Meaning of barbarians? 2. What Paul's further service? 3. What prophecy fulfilled? 5; cf. Mark 16:18; Luke 10:19. What opinion of him? 4, 6; cf. 14:11, 19. How did Paul repay the kindness of the Maltese? 8, 9. What return did they make? 10

4. COMPLETION OF THE SEA VOYAGE, 11b-13. How many different ships from Cæsarea to Puteoli? What points touched after leaving Melita? On Puteoli see C. & H. ii. 351-353.

5. COMPLETION OF THE JOURNEY, 14-16. Why the sojourn at Puteoli? 14. How did the Roman brethren learn of Paul's approach? 15. Over what road did they travel? See C. & H. ii. 354-362. What disposition was made of Paul? 16.

6. PAUL'S PRISON LABORS AT ROME, 17-31.

a. *First Interview with the Jews*, 17-22. Had he met the disciples? 17. How did Paul account for his imprisonment? 17-20. How account for their ignorance of Paul? 21; cf. 22.

b. *Second Interview with the Jews*, 23-29. Character of his discourse? 23; cf. 17:2, 3, etc. Point of the quotation in 26, 27, and the remark in 28?

c. *Two Years' Prison Preaching*, 30, 31. What co-workers? cf. Eph. 6:22; Phil. 1:1; 2:25-30; Col. 4:9, 10, 11-14; Philemon 23, 24. What fruits? Phil. 1:12-18; 4:22. How supported? ch. 28:30; cf. Phil. 4:14-18. Why the abrupt termination of Acts? What inference as to time of composition?

d. *Writes Ephesians, Colossians and Philemon*. Evidence: (1) Tychicus carried Ephesians and Colossians, Eph. 6:21, 22; Col. 4:7, 8. (2) Onesimus carried Philemon, 10-12. (3) The two traveled together, Col. 4:9. (4) Surrounded by same companions, Col. 4:10-14; Philem. 23, 24. (5) A prisoner, Eph. 3:1; 4:1; Col. 4:18; Philem. 1. (6) Only long imprisonment at Cæsarea and Rome. From Cæsarea went to Rome; now expecting to be released and to visit Philemon, 22.

e. *Historical Items in the Three Epistles.* (1) Paul desired opportunity and boldness, Eph. 6:19, 20; Col. 4:2-4. (2) History of Onesimus, Philem. 10-9. Philemon's home? 2; cf. Col. 4:17. (3) Facts about Mark? Col. 4:10; cf. Acts 15:37. (4) A lost epistle, Col. 4:15, 16. Which epistle no personal salutations and why?

f. *Writes Philippians.* Evidence; Paul a prisoner at Rome, 1:12-14; 4:22. Written before or after Ephesians and Colossians? cf. Eph. 6:18-20; Col. 4:3; Phil. 1:12-14; 4:22. How reach the prætorian guard? 1:13; cf. Acts 28:16.

g. *Historical Items in Philippians.* (1) Epistle of love and joy, 1:3-5, 7, 8, 25, 26; 2:1, 2, 17, 18; 3:1; 4:1, 4, 9. (2) Two classes of officers at Philippi, 1:1. (3) His bonds had furthered the cause; how and where? 1:12-18. (4) His case undecided but critical, 1:20, 23; 2:23. (5) Hoping to be released and to visit Philippi, 1:25, 26; 2:24. (6) Expects to send Timothy to Philippi, 2:19-23. (7) Write a history of Epaphroditus from 2:25-30. (8) They had ministered to Paul three times, 4:10-18.

Epistle to the Hebrews.

1. CHARACTERISTICS.

1. Not addressed to particular person or congregation.

2. Author's name not given.

3. Begins and proceeds like a treatise..

4. Epistolary traits in ch. 13.

II. AUTHORSHIP.

1. In early centuries ascribed to (1) Paul, (2) Luke, (3) Barnabas, (4) Clement.

2. Church of Rome (1) once denied, (2) now maintains Paul's authorship.

3. Reformers: (1) Luther ascribed it to Apollos, (2) Calvin to a disciple of Apollos.

4. In favor of Pauline authorship. (1) Written from Italy, 13:24. (2) By an associate of Timothy, 13:23. (3) Writer under restraint but hoping for release, 13:18, 19, 23. (4) Drift of argument is Pauline.

5. Against Pauline authorship. (1) Style more rhetorical. (2) Author received gospel at second hand, 2:4; cf. Gal. 1:11-20. On use of "we" see 2:1; 4:1; 6:1. (3) An Alexandrian hue, i. e. allegorical. But cf. 1 Cor. 10:1-12; Gal. 4:19-31.

III. PERSONS ADDRESSED.

1. Had suffered for the faith and aided the writer and others; 6:10; 10:32-34.

2. Now on verge of apostasy, 2:1-3; 3:12; 5:11; 6:4-9; 10:23-39; 12:25.

3. Had been disciples a long time, 5:12.

4. Had been associated with the writer, 13:19.

5. Timothy about to visit them, 13:23.

6. Were accustomed to Jewish ritual. See whole epistle.

7. Were familiar with lxx. Hence, some body of Jewish Christians in danger of going back to Judaism. Either Palestinian or Alexandrian Jews. In favor of latter, (1) Were liberal benefactors, 6:10; former were recipients of bounty. (2) Had not resisted unto blood, 12-3, 4; former furnished many early martyrs. (3) Style of reasoning better fits Alexandrian culture.

IV. DATE.

Evidently written while the temple was standing and its services going on.

V. ANALYSIS.

1. Argumentative, 1-10:18. Jews urged three points in which Judaism was superior to Christianity.

a. Angel argument; answered in chaps. 1, 2. (1) Jesus higher than angels, yet, (2) a man, and able to sympathize.

b. Moses argument; answered in chaps. 3-4:13. (1) Moses a servant in the house, (2) Jesus a son over the house, (3) Jesus a builder of the house.

c. Priesthood argument, 4:14-10:18. (1) Exhortation, based on anticipated argument, 4:14-16. (2) Character of Jesus' priesthood, 5:1-9. (3) Superiority to Levitical priesthood, 5:10-7:28. (*a*) Order of Melchizedek. (*b*) Priest by oath. (*c*) Hortatory digression, 5:11-6:20. (4) Superiority of *sanctuary* in which, *covenant* under which, and *sacrifice* with which, Christ ministers, 8-10:18.

PAUL'S LATER HISTORY.

1. RELEASE FROM FIRST ROMAN IMPRISONMENT.

Implied, (1) In his expectation, Phil. 1:25, 26; 2:24; Philem. 22. (2) In incidents that do not fit into his earlier life. See epistles to Timothy and Titus. (3) Accords with universal early tradition. See C. & H. ii. 437-439.

2. HISTORICAL ITEMS IN I. TIMOTHY.

a. *Paul Revisits Ephesus and Macedonia*, 1:3. (1) Not the

long stay of Acts 19. Cf. Acts 19:22; 20:1; 1 Tim. 1:3. (2) How reconcile this visit with Acts 20:35? (3) Purpose in visiting Macedonia? cf. Phil. 2:19-24. (4) Place and purpose of the epistle? 1:3; 3:15. (5) Further plans? 3:14. (6) Did he visit Philemon? Philem. 22.

b. *Unsafe Teachers at Ephesus*, 1:3-7; 6:20, 21; cf. Acts 20:29, 30.

c. *Elders to be Compensated*, 5:17, 18. What distinction in elders?

d. *State of Timothy's Health*, 5:23.

3. HISTORICAL ITEMS IN TITUS.

a. *Visits Crete and Leaves Titus*, 1:5. State of Cretans and mission of Titus? 1:5-13.

b. *Goes to Nicopolis, and on the way writes Titus*, 3:12. Where Titus to go? Who to take his place? Who to go with him? 3:13.

4. SECOND ROMAN IMPRISONMENT. (1) Writes II. Timothy, 1:8, 16, 17; 2:8, 9. (2) Deserted in Asia, 1:15. What exception? 1:16-18. (3) Expecting martyrdom, 4:6, 8. (4) Movements of companions? 4:9-13. Was Timothy at Thessalonica, 4:10, or Ephesus, 12, or Troas, 13, or Corinth, 20, or Miletus, 20? (5)

Experience at first trial? 4:16, 17. (6) Last glimpse of old friends, 4:19, 20. Paul probably beheaded in last year of Nero, A. D. 68. Why not crucified?

PETER'S LATER HISTORY.

1. LAST SEEN IN ACTS, 15:7.

2. LATEST CONNECTION WITH PAUL, Gal. 2:11.

3. WRITES FIRST PETER.

a. *From "Babylon,"* 5:13; literal or symbolical?

b. *To Churches in Asia Minor*, 1:1. Jewish or Gentile? cf. 1:14, 21; 2:10; 3:6; 4:3. Sense of "dispersion?" 1:1. Written after Paul's second tour.

c. *Historical Items.* (1) Churches persecuted, 2:12; 3:13, 14; 4:12-19. (2) Epistle sent by Sylvanus (Silas) 5:12. Last previous reference, Acts 18:5; 1 Thess. 1:1; 2 Thess. 1:1. (3) Mark mentioned, 5:13. Peter's "son." Trace his movements in Acts 15:39; Col. 4:10; 2 Tim. 4:11. With Peter between Paul's two imprisonments.

4. WRITES SECOND PETER.

a. *To Same Churches*, 3:1.

b. *Historical Items.* (1) Expecting martyrdom; 1:13-15; cf.

John 21:13-15. (2) Alludes to transfiguration, 1:16-18. (3) Familiar with Paul's Epistles, 3:15, 16. What indication bearing on date?

5. PETER'S DEATH. Early tradition that under Nero he was crucified at Rome, head downward.

JAMES' LATER HISTORY.

1. JAMES, BROTHER OF JOHN, killed by Herod, Acts 12:3.
2. JAMES, BROTHER OF OUR LORD.
   a. *Prominence at Jerusalem*, Acts 15:13; Gal. 1:19.
   b. *Last Bible Reference*, Acts 21:18.
   c. *Traditions of His Death.* (1) Stoned by Sadducees, A. D. 62; Jos. Ant. xx. 9, 1. (2) Thrown from pinnacle of temple by Pharisees, A. D. 69; Euseb., Ecc. History ii. 23.
3. EPISTLE OF JAMES. (1) Which James? 1:1. Opinions differ. Probably the second. (2) Persons addressed, 1:1. Believers or unbelievers? 1:18; 2:1; 4:7, 8.

EPISTLE OF JUDAS.

1. WHAT JUDAS? 1, 17; cf. Mark 6:3; Luke 6:16; Acts 1:13. Probably not an apostle but brother of the James in Mark 6:3.
2. INDICATION OF DATE, 4:17, 18.

JOHN'S LATER HISTORY.

1. DROPS OUT OF ACTS AT 8:14, 25.

2. LATER ALLUSION BY PAUL, Gal. 2:9.

3. HIS WRITINGS.

   a. *Fourth Gospel.*

   b. *Revelation,* 1:1, 2, 4, 9. (1) Date according to Irenæus A. D. 96. (2) Place, 1:9. Why there? (3) Day of week? 1:10. (4) Churches addressed and location? 2:1, 8, 12, 18; 3:1, 7, 14.

   c. *Three Epistles.*

LITERATURE CONSULTED.

CLARK, Harmonic Arrangement of Acts.
CONEYBEARE AND HOWSON. Life and Epistles of St. Paul.
FARRAR, The Story of St. Paul.   Early Days of Christianity.
JACOBUS, Notes on Acts.
HINSDALE, The Jewish Christian Church.
HURLBUT, Manual of Bible History and Geography.
LANGE, The Several Volumes of his Commentary on Acts and the Epistles.
MYER, Commentaries.
MCGARVEY, Commentary on Acts.   Class Book on Acts.   Lands of the Bible.
MCCLINTOCK AND STRONG, Encyclopedia.
MANDER, Planting and Training of the Apostolic Church.
PULPIT COMMENTARY.
PALEY, Horae Paulinæ.
RENAN, Saint Paul.
SMITH, New Testament History.
———— Bible Dictionary.
SCHAFF, History of the Apostolic Church.
SCHAFF-HERTZOG, Encyclopedia.
STALKER, Life of St Paul.
STIFLER, An Introduction to the Study of Acts.
W. M. TAYLOR, Paul the Missionary.
THOMPSON, The Land and the Book.
ZOLLARS, The Holy Day and the Sacred Book.

www.ingramcontent.com/pod-product-compliance
Lightning Source LLC
Chambersburg PA
CBHW031335160426
43196CB00007B/693